The Universal Fundamentals

Integrational Light Energies
The Universal Fundamentals

Order this book online at www.trafford.com
or email orders@trafford.com

Most Trafford titles are also available at major online book retailers.

Printed in the United States of America.

ISBN: 978-1-4269-6342-1 (sc)

Trafford rev. 04/07/2011

www.trafford.com

North America & international
toll-free: 1 888 232 4444 (USA & Canada)
phone: 250 383 6864 ♦ fax: 812 355 4082

Table of Contents

Introduction

The Universal Fundamentals

I am hoping this book will enlighten and help you with your discovery of your inner true self as you grow through your spiritual journey. You will come to an inner quiet space to listen to your heart. You will be able to ask from your heart all that will enlighten you. I am hoping that through your life process of coming to terms with who you really are; you will be able to understand your ascension process and what you aspire to be with God's love and light.

I am writing this book because the knowledge I wish to share with you is now available as we go through transitional changes personally and together with our planet. Many topics of this book are of intense intermediate, advanced spiritual content. It is important to note why these segments are in the sequence they are. They are the building blocks of knowledge and changes as you progress through specific levels of layers, while you are experiencing your integration and upgrade of your being.

We are all on a soul journey and we have experiences that provide us with enhanced opportunities of learning and growing with life's lessons. These lessons can be mental, emotional, physical and spiritual in nature. There is no separation of these light fundamentals because each is interconnected and work in alignment with each other.

I am offering you an insightful perception into how and why everything is connected and interconnected through various levels of your core being and how this builds spiritual light bridges to higher levels of consciousnesses of light and love.

The knowledge and experiences that I write about relate to the understanding, processing, experiencing, and changing within, of re-building, and re-creating a new life blueprint while we retain our current physical body.

This is a new creation process called "ascension" and with the assistance of the Light Hierarchies of the Universe, Angels, Ascended Masters and Teachers sent by God as we change in light and form.

They have always been there watching and waiting for each soul to begin to consciously "awaken within" for aeons. They are of the highest hierarchy in relation to the existence of the universal laws.

The two laws of non-interference and soul evolution, were strictly maintained for our benefit over aeons as we are given all the time needed to learn and grow: mentally, emotionally, physically, spiritually and ethereally.

It is now different and new because before we would go home to create a new life chart of our next incarnation with our ethereal light body. The ascension process allows the changes to occur through mind, body and spirit while we are occupying a physical body.

We will feel the changes more, because we have the light bodies to integrate while in a physical body. Where as, when we were home we would only have our spirit light body and the changes were much easier to transition through.

The ascension begins with the new light infusion process within our cellular genetic makeup. It then progresses into re-building of DNA and RNA matrix strains, while we simultaneously become aware of the need to undergo the process of making conscious connections to facilitate the cleaning, cleaning and releasing process within our light bodies.

The light bodies are the emotional, physical, spiritual and ethereal. We are introduced to the knowledge of these light mechanisms. Our spiritual learning is to understand how each one operates within us and begin to take responsibility of facilitating our own inner house cleaning.

We are to learn the conscious realization of acknowledging, accepting, and releasing what we no longer need or want, while each key lesson is stored within our soul's light chart. With the realization of cleaning and clearing out the junk of our light bodies, our inner core light is able to emerge as the light it is. We are actually attuning our inner core light to match our higher twin self.

We cannot progress unless we move beyond the mental, emotional, and physical confines that have held us in illusions. The illusions are the ego mind, fears, the emotions and the physical attachments.

Before the process begins we must clear all karma, these include all lessons in past lives, and present. Then we must learn how our light bodies work within us, in order to acknowledge our lessons and the teachings we needed to learn.

Once we are able to connect to these experiences, we then learn how to let go of all attachments so we can move forward towards our ascension process. Once we achieve this level of awareness, we then receive spiritual teachings and the gift of mastering a new life service with unconditional love for self, others, and with divinity.

These segments will describe the ascension process as well as all the layers of sub-systems, energy centers and your core being within you, as you go through tremendous life altering conscious connections with all these. You will feel it within every aspect of you while simultaneously upgrading your levels of awareness and consciousness. Your life will reflect the changes you have made.

My life started to change slowly since 2002. I was given a choice to go home or continue on the path being set for me to go through. I was given six weeks to come to terms with my family, my life and myself. The morning of my surgery, I was at complete peace and I surrendered to God's path for me.

I survived cervical cancer only finding out weeks ahead of this diagnosis. Thankfully, I have chosen to fulfill every necessary task that will take place over the next several years to come. We all have continuous key reference points in life in which lessons and love have begun or will begin or have ended.

My next life moment began in 2006. It was a typical January morning, the air was crisp and cool and I had a difficult night sleeping as I was awakened by the gentle voice of my guardian angel. I was told of another life-changing event that would be coming for me.

I spent half of the night in deep thought and time slipped away; what seemed like hours, passed in only a few moments. I decided to take a walk before I started my workday.

While on my walk, I was thinking about the night before and the soft gentle voice that had awoken me and whispered to me that my husband was going home. I was trying to understand the reason behind why this was going to happen to my children and me. Tears and snowflakes fell slowly down my cheeks as I started back home to begin my workday.

For several months before my husband would go peacefully into the light, I am blessed with the increasing presence of my guardian angel and my loved ones in spirit.

I could feel God's presence through this whole life changing experience not just for my children and me but also for my beloved husband. I knew that I could not share my knowledge of my husband's passing with him as he would not understand nor comprehend what was going to become of his living spirit.

I understood the change was coming as he made his choice to return home. I spent many waking months and hours reassuring him that I was there to support and love him unconditionally. In fact, I did this for him during the thirteen years we were married, as he needed me in many other ways not related to his health. During the last few days together, I felt that the change was going to happen.

My husband never spoke of believing in afterlife but believed in heaven and God. He made it a point of letting me know unexpectedly that he loved me and thanked me shortly before he made his transition.

My beloved husband suddenly passed within hours of that moment. I was stunned and shocked. Even knowing it was going to come, did not make the loss any easier when it happened.

This is not the first time I have known of those close to me going to make the transition, but this was certainly the most personally challenging trial for me to face, live with and behold my faith. I was now a single mom and I had two young children to care for.

Every lesson whether painful or joyful is a choice we make with others or we choose to experience it. These experiences are already outlaid what is not known is our response to it and how we handle it. The learning experience does not know what is coming for our benefit out of love.

I realized that my beloved husband transition was one out of love for me and for him. What may seem difficult to understand is why, when this happens to you feel for the love and compassion from them. Grief, pain, anger, and sadness cover the light of truth and love. We being human have to content with emotions, but we have a choice which emotions to feel and express. That is even a lesson in itself.

What ever we have chosen to go through, we need to journey through it to see the pure lesson of love and attain a better understanding of it.

For every ending, there is a beginning, even in the mist of our trials and tribulations. Be still for clarity, truth, and illumination of your heart.

Be

Real

Free

Pure

Wonder

Believe

Segment I
Being You

Being You

You are your past, present and future. You have the gift of choosing better conscious loving choices that will allow your potential to flourish on your spiritual journey. I have always felt that we are here for a higher purpose. I came into my life being aware of the spiritual side of life and knowing that we are never alone. It has been said that when we are born our memories of our original state of being are blocked so that we can learn and complete our soul's contracts.

We all have an inner voice that guides us along on our journey and our life experiences; we become aware of this during our moments of reflection and thinking, "now what? How do I handle this? What can I do to learn and grow with this?" This of course depends on the situation you are dealing with. We all have an inner wiser voice that guides us through our challenges we have a choice to listen to this.

I feel we all have this deep desire to understand who and what we really are. What is life really about? Some people feel more connected to this truth. This is of their spiritual connection with God. Our true light essence and spirit will eventually emerge, because our soul knows of home. Our soul is accompanying us on our continuous journey of change and growth.

We all have a soul and we can choose to acknowledge it or not. Regardless of what we choose to believe, our higher self compels us to move through our challenges and trials.

Have you had times when you just want to be alone with yourself or take a walk and just want to clear your head and just be quiet?

These are your precious moments to find, listen and feel within you, which are giving you guidance to whatever situation or feeling you are having. You are giving yourself the required processing time that brings clarity and truth.

Your experiences in this life are important stepping-stones as they define your lessons of learning and the characteristics that make you who you are. This is also true with past lives that you have lived before. Many like to call this reincarnation. What ever you believe, we have abundance from divinity with love. Gratitude and love of God, opens us to all perceptions and infinite possibilities. This is an essential element of building spiritual bridges within us. These spiritual bridges allow us to tap into increasing self-awareness and continuous creative expression of ourselves. Once we create these inner bridges we open up to deeper spiritual enlightenment and truth that is available to us, at the pace and understanding we can comprehend.

Do we really put enough time into the investment of our own self? Our lives mirror our choices and thoughts. In order to bring change about, you must become the change you wish to be and for others to see.

Life is about making positive changes, adapting, learning, sharing, and growing. The choices of one or more people can directly affect the direction of others and events of life. We are to discern which choices enhance life for all.

Are you going through changes in your lifestyle, your job, family, your very being? Do you feel that life is passing by you, around you and you are trying to make sense of it?

This is a good starting point, to deal with any baggage that you might be carrying around with you. With time and a conscious effort, you will understand the past, present and future and how they have shaped you. They are the experiences that directly or indirectly now define you. In order to go forward, you may need to look back and resolve issues.

This is an exercise in realizing what happened then. How it affected you. How it shaped you. What can you change about you?

Exercise:
Write a list of all of your childhood memories both the good and the challenging times.
What memories are relevant?
Then write down how you handled each experience and how you reacted to them.

The reason of this exercise above is to recapture your inner connection to your light of wonder, purity and joy. Your child hood memories of your experiences and those you had around you cannot diminish your light. You have the ability to see through your experiences objectively and detach the emotional and physical parameters that may have covered your innocence.

Imagine recapturing a delightful experience as a child and holding on that moment of joy. It can be anything that brought a moment of love and inner peace. I have fond memories of first snowfalls and just wanting to walk and play in it. The feeling of being in that moment allows your heart to be and your mind is a quiet serene like a blanket of white fresh snow.

Do you remember your childhood dreams? What did you dream of becoming? What was your inner voice saying to you as a child? You are able to retrieve these moments of your true self. You are able to go back and find your inner child innocence, by remembering that part which is in you.

As a child, I often walked and played in the forests that were around my home. I would go to the park, look up to the sky, remember, and feel the connection of purpose of my life. Even then, I did not fully understand what it was but it was there and someday I would know.

Throughout my childhood experiences, that part of innocence and purity in me never separated from me but was a constant companion as I played and learnt through my lessons. No matter what you may have been through you always have this part within you that knows and feels in this place of me is God's unconditional love and presence.

As you are able to understand more of you through your childhood the following exercise is helpful to understanding who you are today.

Exercise:
Are there any relevant patterns of behaviour you can associate with today in your life style?
What have been your life choices do they reflect those who were or are still part of your life?
Are you still dealing with childhood memories and experiences that you have not dealt with or chosen to forget because of the feelings it created?
What are they?
Why do you think you have them?

Wisdom

Grace

Appreciation

Understanding

Humility

Forgiveness

Segment II
Karma and Lessons Learnt

Karma and Lessons Learnt

In this chapter, I will talk about the importance of clearing all karma and retaining the lessons you have learnt. This will take you to your next step and what the higher self's guidance is impressing upon you. It is important to understand that in order to clear your present self, it is essential to clear your past karma.

Your past lives carry karma that has helped you. It is like going through school where you have experiences and learnt lessons along the way. What is important is to recognize any key lessons, triggers, or experiences that you are still carrying within from past lives. It is possible to carry remaining experiences and lessons into your present life so that you accept the opportunity to apply wisdom to these. Wisdom erases karma.

Are you carrying these experiences with you still? What do you need to learn? What do you need to let go of now? What have you accomplished? What did you go through? The answers to these questions will help you understand these integrated parts of you.

We all have within us the tools needed to come to assist with our soul's journey thus far. These tools are of truth, clarity, love, trust, and peace that transmute through the mental, emotional, and physical light bodies that connect us to the truth of how life is, balanced, understood, and cherished.

These light bodies are light filters. We cannot separate one from the other; they rely on each other as a child does their mother and father.

For example, there is a child named Rick who is envious of another child, Jimmy, who just got a new red shiny bicycle. Rick runs into his house looking for his mom, and he asks if he can have a new bike like Jimmy's, and his mother says no. She says, "Rick you have a nice bike right now, you don't need a new one yet." Now, guess what Rick is going to say, feel and do about this? Rick is not going to give up, but rather he is going to find dad to ask him. Rick with his child-like innocence and joy runs off to find dad. Dad was in the shed cleaning it out getting ready for yard work. Rick asks dad, "Daddy can I have a new bike like Jimmy's? Dad says to Rick, "No you cannot have a new bike. Your bike is fine."

Rick thought dad would say yes even though his mother said no. Rick becomes upset that he is not getting a new bike. Rick's dad said, "Let's wash your bike and see if it needs any fixing up." Rick said, "No I want a new bike now!" Rick was angry and upset and could only think about a new bike. Rick, now expressing his feelings and emotions ran up to his room to sulk. Mom and dad know why he cannot have a new bike because Rick is not big enough to ride a bike like Jimmy's. Rick does not understand this, but only wants what he could see. Rick has to grow and learn to ride his own bike better before he was ready for a new bigger bike.

We can apply this lesson in relation to our spiritual growth and becoming more aware as we continue to learn with the experiences that are to come. Prayer works the same way with our God. When we ask or pray do we get what we want? This depends whether it is right for us. Can we handle it?

Is it for the right reasons? Do we have the right tools and learnt skills?

The place and stage we are at with karma will allow us to grow from the sub-consciousness to the conscious level. Understanding your past blueprint karma and your past lives, will assist in the transition between these two levels of consciousness and will then connect you to your enhanced and expanded conscious level that will become your focus. Past karma is a gift of re-experience and lessons that move us forward.

What steps do you take to do this? Maybe you know already and you are at the point of starting to discover your past and your karma.

Suggested steps to begin:

Writing a daily journal about how you feel.
What do you want to know?
Learn how to meditate.
Take time just for you with no distractions.
Learn how to remember your dreams.
Write down your dreams.

Exercise:
Reflect on your life experiences.
What have you learnt?
What fears and phobias are holding you back?
What do you dream?
Do you understand your dreams?
Are you aware of your past lives?
Do you have moments of déjà vu with people and places?

As you attempt to understand yourself better and clear yourself of your childhood experiences and your present self, your understanding and awareness of your past lives will surface. You can experience your past lives in dreams. You can even do this with meditation that allows you the time of inner quiet to see and listen.

As your state of conscious awareness increases and develops more in your dreams you can see where, when, feel, connect and heal past lives. You are being an active participant in understanding and healing your past lives.

Your karma attached to those life times will surface and you will have the opportunity to apply your wisdom to those lifetimes and erase your karma. You will retain your lessons and your spiritual growth of those times.

Your guides will help you understand how to clear karma. Your awareness of your past lives will then move into your subconscious. As you create spiritual bridges between your subconscious and conscious states, you will apply your higher self's wisdom to your life times.

How do you know if you are clearing your karma? Your types of life experiences and choices will change as you change. You will begin to understand your higher self and your heart as you open up to more spiritual understanding and awareness. As you define your conscious choices, you will feel as you are lighter and at more content with you. Your choices will reflect what you choose to seek that brings you inline with your heart.

Strength

Courage

Endurance

Acknowledge

Appreciate

Gratitude

Segment III
Re-Connective Healing

Re-Connective Healing

You can do re-connective healing while you become consciously aware of your past lives and karma while in your conscious or dream state. Your guides will allow you to go into your specific past lives to do re-connective healing if needed. You will see the specific lessons and those who were part of that life and why.

As you learn how to do re-connective healing, those souls you have encountered will feel the effects of your willingness to transform karma in each past life. Re-connective healing of your past and your karma will enlighten your heart.

About a year and a half after my beloved husband transitioned, I received the blessing of the knowledge and insight of realizing I had seven lifetimes with him. This is when God blessed me with the knowledge and insight of our past lives together.

At this point, I became aware of re-connective healing, as I accepted the opportunity to heal and experience all of my past lives with my husband. I spent a lot of time in prayer as I was coming to terms with my grief process and beginning my life anew. I knew I was going to be fine and that my husband was healing on the other side.

It is a blessing knowing that the moments before we separated with each other we were allowed our time to understand the love God has for each of us. The re-connective healing not only brought the love and light that we both received, but I understood why and my grief lifted. We are not separated. "God stepped in to love and heal his spirit."

I came to the realization that in fact all of my lessons and trials in this lifetime were opportunities to do re-connective healing of any past lives and karma. I have had souls who were part of my past who needed healing receive it and were released I am aware of specific past lives and experiences because I had to clear them in this lifetime.

Re-connective healing is a light heart spiritual energy we all have. It activates by our realization of taking responsibility to our past, karma, all situations, all experiences, and all those we met and meet with wisdom and grace. We can heal others and ourselves emotionally, physically, spiritually with re-connective healing only through the heart.

We have the opportunity to use wisdom with this healing for our world and everything in it. There is now an opportunity for mother nature to heal her planet. God created this world for us to live in peace and to share and respect all its inter-connective systems.

Are you only now realizing and experiencing the repercussions of our misuses of the natural resources of our world that have affected mother nature's delegate nature of balance? Take the responsibility for the conditions you have created by your self-ego choices. We have been given great wisdom and responsibility what have we done with these?

The list of miscorrelations is long and you only need to look at how our world has been shaped around humanity's ego, emotional and physical needs that serve these illusions. To begin re-connective healing with our planet we are to purge all lower ego energies, which cannot exist anymore with our planet and us.

These lower self-based ego energies have hurt a great number of people in many ways; countries and people driven into despair at the expense of others profiting through their egos and the millions of souls who lost their lives at the hand of millennia of wars

We are co-dependent on mother nature and she is now purging our misappropriations of her natural resources. God gives all his children unconditional love and always offers us the chance to get things right. Re-connective healing occurs on a personal, spiritual, karmic, and planetary level. Compassion brings us closer to understanding love. We all have this within us because we all come from love and light.

Over the next several years to come, you will bear witness to the transformation of global re-connective healing. You have many choices of love, choose wisely.

You have the gift of healing your inner heart, you are to take that responsibility first before you can have other creative opportunities. "God says to all his children of light, see within your hearts my light and wisdom. You are not the only expression of my love."

There are many forms of re-connective healing on earth, which mother nature provides. These are all the animals, all plant life and the source and life of your waters. Mother nature has been caring for all of these parts of life too, we have not been sharing with in harmony and balance. We have taken too much from her natural resources that offer balance to all life. We are not allowed to take anymore of her resources; she will protect her life systems by cleansing, purging and re-balancing all life.

Animals have a natural and pure form of re-connective healing that softens our hearts. When our hearts are open, we can feel their unconditional love. All animals are of pure light and they give it freely. All they ask is that they are cared for and loved in return.

For example, dogs offer us love in many ways such as companionship, guidance with earth duties, comfort they love with undivided loyalty, and they play with us. This applies to all animals be it: cats, horses, birds, dolphins and so on. You have all the splendour to feel and be in harmony with all mother nature's animals.

We have many beautiful lands, trees, plants and flowers that are all over our world. We are gifted with the five senses to enjoy this colourful array of beauty and perfection. It is all around us and if we spend more time connected to this beauty of nature, we will truly understand the harmony and balance of seeing colour, hearing sound, feeling, touching and smelling the life that is shared with us.

Our most important natural resource is our waters. These are the elixirs of life giving properties for all life on our planet. They too offer to us the beauty and life flowing array of essence. Mother nature endlessly replenishes these reservoirs by atmosphere pressures that cause rainfalls. We enjoy mother nature's display of waterfalls to snowfalls. We are to play and share the life-giving gift.

We are to respect, love all that is here to share, treat it as cherished and be responsible with how we interact with all that mother nature provides.

Heal

Comprehend

Accountably

Co-Dependant

Harmony

Balance

Segment IV
The Laws of Unification

The Laws of Unification

Whether we are aware of these Universal Laws or not, they bring harmony and balance from within, and to the life, we are experiencing as well for all universal life. These laws give us the opportunity to learn with wisdom how creation is through mind, heart and soul. These twenty laws govern our ideal choices of love, balance and harmony.

1. The Law of Harmony is the state of joy, peace and unconditional love of self and others. Whenever you act with pure intent, you create light and love that flows abundantly everywhere.

2. The Law of Karma and Reincarnation is the actions, thoughts, emotions, words, deeds, and the motive based on the ego mind and of the physical realm. Karma is the disharmonious state that asks us to apply wisdom and grace within and to acknowledge and accept it through reincarnation.

3. The Law of Wisdom is the state of detachment through the process of acquired experiences, of learnt lessons, and lifetimes with inner knowing of how and what Karma is.

4. The Law of Grace is the mercy you give unconditionally through learnt karma to yourself while extending grace onto others as they clear their Karma.

5. The Law of Soul Evolution is when learning and growth naturally progress to the next state of awareness.

6. The Law of Master is when certain souls who have mastered lifetimes and have cleared all karma, dedicate their light, wisdom and teachings to help others unconditionally in all dimensional facets of life.

7. The Law of Energy Vibration Attainment is the creation of matter and light with thought of harmonious energies into manifestation from divine source.

8. The Law of Free Will is Universal and God given expression of choice that a soul wishes to be or attain for enrichment of soul enlightenment. This law and gift is the divine right of freedom to all souls with the respect of free will of choice.

9. The Law of One is the spark of love and life that exists in all creation from God throughout non-linear time, Universes, and all souls.

10. The Law of Manifestation is that which creates with love and pure intent, which shall bring in more light and truth. Any thought or idea that is lower than the higher self, manifests lessons and Karma.

11. The Law of Conscious Detachment is applying the wisdom of knowing what you cannot change, respect to free will, and detachment of the physical and emotional boundaries to enlighten. Focus on love and light within all and one everywhere.

12. The Law of Gratitude in respect to the Laws of Karma and One is the more you allow God's light to flow through your heart, you will receive the gratitude with wisdom.

13. The Law of Fellowship is when two or more gather for the same purpose the attainment is amplified, doubled, and more.

14. The Law of Resistance is that lesson of learning that you chose to overcome in respect to Karma.

15. The Law of Attraction is what you focus and direct your energies to; you shall reap the fruits of your endeavours.

16. The Law of Reflection is applying your wisdom learnt where your hearts masters how to be of unconditional light.

17. The Law of Unconditional Love is accepting yourself and others as they are without judgements or expectations.

18. The Law of Magnetic Affinities is when a soul and their soul's contract choose a time and place to honour their purpose.

19. The Law of Abundance is the perception within you and from the Universe of how abundance manifests.

20. The Law of Divine Order is the natural balance of nature, energy and all life forms in harmonious unison.

The understanding and knowledge of these laws with lifetime experiences and your choices are with you as you create a new level of expression into your current life chart.

Your guides, your light counsel, the angels and light beings sent by God are helping you to expand your choices as you go through your ascension process.

As I mentioned before all thoughts are energy in creation. If we break these down a pure understanding of being aware of what we create manifests. It is imperative to recognise the inner illusions we have and not apply those to creation of any idea or situation but to learn to let these go through detachment.

What are the illusions that we can detach from, that do not serve you, anyone or God? Illusions delay our potential or experience to achieve harmony and balance. Love transmutes all illusions, fears, and doubts; surrendering and trusting in your true self and the Universe that all that is light and love through change.

The mind, how we process thoughts, actions and expectations depend on the awareness of our ego. With the ascension process, we have to learn to put the ego on the back fence and work through the heart. I am sure you know the expression follow your heart not your head. It takes re-training of the mind to let the ego go, when you are going through the processes of thinking through an idea, thought, situation, or choice.

Emotions and feelings are the part of us that govern self-expression.

How we react, handle and deal with these emotions and feelings is the learning we need to experience to bring us closer to understanding them. These determine the outcome of what we are processing and manifesting. The challenging part is being in balance and harmony with thoughts and ideas.

All thoughts of the mind and ego, feelings, behaviours, and reactions go through the mental process within us first, and then the result is physical. Example: when you experience love and anger, which do you feel is healthier for the body? Negative feelings, thoughts, and actions can make you physically ill as directly related to the thought. Forgiveness of self and others is one way to begin healing. All lower and negative energies transform into physical experiences.

It transmutes the effects of emotional, mental, and the spiritual well-being within us. We have the awareness of understanding, processing, and being within harmonious energies. What we believe to be true amplifies the manifestation into creation as well. If we believe in ourselves, our ideas trust others and want a better joyful world it will become reality. This principal thus brings us into applying the action that brings change.

Everything from the mind except the ego, thoughts, feelings, ideas, and experiences, transcends to the physical then connects to the spiritual then to the ethereal light. God knows all. Through positive change, more self-awareness, wisdom, strength, courage, honesty, humility, grace and acceptance, we learn the importance of applying the Universal Laws for our harmonious potential. These Universal Laws are within you and as you grow in spiritual awareness of these, your light bodies will apply the principles you have learnt with mind, body and spirit. Manifestation of divine purpose will begin to shape your inner, and outer world and with the Universe simultaneously.

Can you re-shape your life without the understanding of these Universal Laws in your heart?

The Universe we are part of instinctively knows of these divine laws of unification. God has many forms of creation all part of the greater expression of life that span across our Universe and others.

Our planet has been created by God's divine expression of co-creation. Mother nature honours and cherishes these laws of unification. All animals, all plant life, and our natural resources abide by these laws.

Humanity has misused these laws for self-ego purposes, and for fear based illusions of the mind. The physical ramifications of what has been created by humanity have been to accommodate these illusions. This has changed the delicate nature of balance that was initially created long ago.

God has given us these laws not only within our hearts but also with the testaments of creation and revelations in the Holy Bible. This book is the word and love of God. The Bible is available in many languages for all faiths to open the minds and hearts of God's children.

God and mother nature will not allow Humanity to continue in using gifts of creation unless it is for balance and harmony for all life.

Humanity's lesson of wisdom and grace is to understand the gifts that God has bestowed upon them. We are meant to co-exist and create with God's will. The lessons and trials of humanity are those that you have created, are creating these are not of divine will.

Harmony

Stability

Sharing

Expressive

Creating

Love

Segment V
States of Consciousness

States of Consciousness

We all have states of consciousness that work in unison. These include the unconscious, super-conscious and the conscious state. We often tap into the unconscious and the super conscious through dream awareness and meditation. Dreams bring experiences, feelings, and triggers about a situation to the surface so we can perceive what we are ready to release or face with grace and humility.

As with spiritual growth, the nature of dreams goes through transitional phases. As the mind opens up to the conscious connection of increasing self awareness it changes the persona of our dream types and meditative states, and deepens our own personal and spiritual connection of ourselves and with God. The key to becoming aware of the messages given to you is becoming aware of your soul's truth within you.

The subconscious is a tool that brings up feelings, emotions, situations, and people in our dream or meditative state. The subconscious relays what we have created by our current perceptions of attachments to that give meaning and purpose in our lives.

The three levels of consciousnesses that we are aware of are about are all matrixes of energies and light patterns that are attached to the ego, emotional and physical parameters based life here of the third realm.

What and how you perceive things is by living through your awareness of choices presented to you.

We are reminded to remember the Universal perspective; the grand scale of how energies work through these states in order to see the bigger picture of life. As we become aware of how these states act within us, we have the choice and ability to perceive more about life.

I recommend you start a dream journal. It is a good idea to write things down so you are aware of what your subconscious is telling you through your dream state. Even if you cannot remember your dreams, we have the wonderful gift in the mind to re-train ourselves to recall and release. If we can expand our awareness through sleep, imagine being able to do it in a conscious state!

The interesting part is recognising what the subconscious is relaying; we can tell it to bring these messages into our conscious state. This is re-conditioning your inner states to your natural state of being. You can become a conscious and active participant in your spiritual evolvement.

Once you are able to do this, you can apply this technique to becoming aware of your past lives, karma, and receiving higher teaching and knowledge, as you move more into being an active participant.

As a child, I always dreamt of premonitions and interacted with the spiritual realm. I often felt those I loved and knew me were close. My first moment of consciousness and being aware of home was my transitional birth into this lifetime.

This memory is still with me as I was in conscious awareness with the other side.

I am thankful of this a gift because I have the conscious ethereal awareness of home with me. Whether you are aware of it or not it is just fine. There is no wrong or right. Life is about making and becoming the choices that feel right for you.

God has blessed me with the conscious connection of home for his purpose. I have known since a young child of six that I was part of a plan to come. I started my inner healing work at the age of three, but became aware of it at six. I began at six working with the dimensional light portals and I continued to do this for many years. I kept a lot of my spiritual side quiet as a child but often spoke up about the premonitions I was having.

The challenging part is figuring out what is what, how it works, and experiencing these various conscious states and it helps you along your spiritual journey of discovering you. I have been working with this a long time and find it amazing what and how thought can limit or expand our perception of these states.

As you begin to discover and take the time to work and understand these conscious states, you will eventually realize there are more states beyond the third realm.

As we learn, grow and evolve with these conscious states we will be gifted with increasing conscious awareness of how the Universe and all life are connected. You will be able to realize where you are in your spiritual evolution as a conscious being. The next step in your consciously development is up to you and where you choose to be by your conscious awareness. Within all these states there is a part of us that seeks the light.

We all have that ability and wisdom to see the light in our hearts. This light is all around us, with each other, and even in the unconscious state. We can choose to acknowledge truths of wisdom and love. These truths are available to all who want to be aware of the Universal connection to consciousness.

The Universe is a conscious living creative expression of life and form. Mother nature is a living conscious creative expression of life energies. God connects to all of creation with consciousnesses, they are specific as unique as they are.

What a wonderful gift humanity has to become aware of God's connection to each of us and all with consciousness. Imagine humanity's potential through maturity, wisdom, love and grace with this awareness.

Your conscious state creates and manifests your thoughts.
What are you creating for yourself?
What are you choosing through your unconscious state?
Are you aware of inner conscious connection to your heart?
Are you aware of your higher self in a conscious state?
Are you aware of your guides and their guidance?

As you learn to understand how all three states are parts of you through your experiences, you will be able to discern the differences of each and see your truth.

Your spiritual expansion of awareness is beginning when you create your inner bridges of your conscious state in your dream states and the super conscious connection with God and the Universe.

Conscious

Potential

Connect

Understand

Universal

Divine

Segment VI

Consciousness is Energy Expanding

Consciousness Is Energy Expanding

We are conscious life force that wishes to co-create with spirit. We are at the beginning stages of realizing our potential as light with the development of conscious maturity that will come. God created us with a conscious connection to him with our spirit. When we realize how to awaken our hearts, we will feel this understanding and presence with us. What an incredible gift we have with God, a heart connection through spirit.

Conscious energy has patterns, colours, frequencies, and varying levels of degrees of specializations. We each have our own unique pattern, frequency, which is reflective to our soul's light energy. God designs these for our part of his divine plan.

We are to discern our free will for betterment of ourselves and for the oneness of us all. Creation of life means to create life with love while retaining the purest, highest intention of our higher self while consciously connect to all and to share with an open heart. Entrusted with so much, we are to apply wisdom through learnt karma, be responsible, and be an active, willing, conscious participant in our evolution.

Conscious energy provides the building blocks of life, which can either create harmony or create disharmony. We do it every moment whether we are aware of it or not. We are beginning to learn to be aware of how free will and divine will unfold to enlighten our choices.

What are you manifesting through your intentions? Whether you are aware of it or not the answer is within your heart. This is where you will feel your truth and much more! There are no mistakes with choices, intention, and wisdom.

Life can create for the enrichment for all and with inner awareness of understanding all Universal life. As a mass consciousness, the hope of humanity is to now consciously becoming aware of the misuse of freewill, thoughts, and actions. Look at what is happening now around you; watch, see, feel and start change anew.

This process started just over a decade ago by light workers who put light energy connectors in place around the world to bring about changes for our planet and for us. Positive and pure energies from many around the world have activated these connectors called energy grids. These grids are beacons of light and energy that work simultaneously with us, with mother nature and High Evolutionary Light Counsels from God.

Our conscious energies are moving, discovering, learning, growing, sharing, changing, and absorbing light so we can merge our pure highest intention as a collective mass of a race, to manifest as part of God's divine blueprint for all souls of light and love. We are being reconditioned to let go of I, me, and mine to become we, us, and one.

With or without full awareness we are being asked to change and let go of these subsystems. With time, you will become aware of the understanding of why.

Mother nature is doing her part to release and cleanse our earth of our misappropriation of our choices and our actions.

Humanity will feel the changes on all levels, emotionally, mentally, physically, spiritually and ethereally in order to learn. The ascension process has already begun, it is through these changes that will "hopefully" bring a greater of understanding and maturity for humanity.

The first group of light workers on this planet have completed their ascension process in order to make way for more souls to begin their process and so on. Each soul will transition through their chosen ascension process at the proper time.

What each soul chooses with their understanding of their perception of how they consciousness manifest through the heart so shall they create by experiences.

Humanity has a gift of connecting, creating and becoming one through and with God's love and light. We all have a gift that is within each heart. Once humanity opens to the understanding of consciousness within the heart, the lessons of wisdom and grace become.

This awareness of humanity's gifts instigate soul by soul. Your awareness of your inner heart has a consciousness that offers guidance and wisdom with your understanding. In this knowing of this inner space of listening, feeling and being, you create spiritual bridges of the understanding of the gifts bestowed upon you. These gifts of consciousness are to share, learn, and understand how to co-exist with all.

Your inner awareness of your heart begins with your willingness to let go of your desires, your wishes, your ego thoughts, and to sincerely seek God's light and wisdom. The conscious connection we have with God offers this awareness's of truth and light that the heart understands. The gifts within the gifts of the heart will unfold in time with your faith, trust and patience.

As I mentioned before this conscious awareness develops over life times of lessons learnt. This applies with karma as we learn and remember consciously, the unconscious chosen choices change. The choices you make can bring you closer to realizing your understanding of your light's potential.

Our souls evolve with learnt lessons of the heart and with this conscious awareness of them. With diligence and loving endurance to see and experience lessons of the heart, a greater awareness of your heart emerges. The conscious awareness of letting go of I to us brings change. Your heart has a truth that seeks to be heard and felt. You have the natural ability to choose to awaken your heart and discover the conscious gifts you have with your light. These gifts of your inner light are naturally unfolded and shared with all.

God's expression of light and love includes the awareness of the conscious heart and our soul. What we become with that wisdom and awareness is the beginning of divine will.

The Universe is expanding beyond what we can comprehend right now with this heart conscious awareness. In time the clarity of this understanding and awareness will be shared when we are ready and not before.

Sincerity

Direct

Prospective

Fulfilment

Silent

Open

Segment VII
The Crystal Chakras

The Crystal Chakras

Within each of us we have the life centers of energy that align us with all facets of creation on all levels consisting of: the higher consciousness, a center of pure wisdom, an inner insight of intuition, a center of truth and communication, a center of movement, health and vitality. These are the primary seventh chakra system. They are also the wheels of integrated sub-systems of life energy force, which function within the emotional, mind, and the physical bodies.

The new light crystalline system is located within our new light field. Our light body activates the new light crystal system. It is then integrated into our existing physical body. These light crystals are created with the new light infusion that we are absorbing continuously. They will activate through specific frequencies of light and with our light body. The new crystalline chakra system is an evolutionary system that continues to expand congruent with the Universe as we connect more to this light system. The new crystalline chakra system works with Universal Light Language.

First, we have seven primary energy centers within our physical body. The new crystalline chakras are infused slowly through your crown chakra. The first new chakra activated is called the soul star or the eighth crystal. The new eighth chakra activates by our connection to our higher self and spiritual conscious awareness.

The new light chakra system activates five above our crown chakra, five chakras between the throat to the root chakras and five below our root chakra.

As we go through the integration process of these new crystal chakras within our physical body, our growth and connection to our true self becomes more apparent.

In order to become aware of moving beyond the third dimension we have presently focused on, we need a new light system to allow us to understand and help us become aware of the other existing dimensional shifts and the higher levels of light and truth.

These are the primary centers of the activation of the new crystal light system introduced by your light body:

1. The Soul Star- New Eighth Chakra: This area is where the first new crystalline crystal activates so you can begin to understand your higher self. It is located upper right back of your head.

2. The Pineal and Medulla Areas: The light crystals located here activate after the opening of your new eighth chakra. The pineal and medulla crystals allow you to establish and process the Universal Light Language as light decoder cells. These then establish more of a link with your higher self.

3. The Hypothalamus: This is the center where a fourth crystal activates to allow you to decode the light language cells from the pineal and medulla and gives you understanding and knowledge.

4. New Heart Light Crystal Center: This is the new place to facilitate light energy exchange, sending and receiving light, love and to connect with God and the Universe.

5. The Sacral Center of Universal Creation: This is a sacred place for creation by divinity and honour.

6. New Mother Earth Crystal Receptor: This new crystal allows us to understand our connection to Mother Earth and her life systems.

These new crystal chakras are much finer and more refined to specific light and energy levels. They look like crystals, gems and or rods that align themselves between each existing chakra. When you are ready, they will activate within you to assist you with understanding your light body, which will assist you in making your changes.

The new crystalline chakras in our light field have cell light receptors and transmitters where the activations take place throughout your mind, physical and spiritual light body.

With the new additional crystalline chakra system, the silver cord we all have will change in light transparency and merge with our light body. This will eventually become our new mechanism of light travel. We then will learn how to use to our new light body to travel to expanded levels of awareness, of teaching, learning, and if allowed inter-dimensional experiences.

These will eventually be the main light system we operate from while in a physical body. The introduction of this new light language system takes duration of time to incorporate into our physical body. The new chakras are integrated slowly and gently as we adjust with them as they do connect to our substantial life systems.

The new crystalline chakra system is an evolutionary light language system that continues to expand in congruency to the Universal expression of life. This new system balances and enhances the mind and new light body energies for our higher twin self and our soul's evolution.

We are presented with a unique sequence of passages towards awareness and truth. It is important to understand how the first seven chakras function. It may be useful to explore additional resource material through books, interest or holistic practitioners.

You will be assigned a counsel of light as you go through your Ascension process once you have activated your light body and your new light crystal centers. They will monitor each step of your change emotionally, physically, spiritually. They will also monitor your light body as you make the adjustments of releasing density as you absorb more light.

The crown chakra is where the new DNA and RNA strains are reconnected. Ten of your matrix strains will begin their changes; two of these light matrixes are kept in place so you can do your earthly duties.

This is a time of trust and beholding your faith, as you will feel these activated within you while you are clearing and releasing within your light bodies too.

It is perfectly normal to be aware of seeing, feeling or hearing your light team working with you throughout your upgrade. This re-coding, re-programming and re-alignment process of your new DNA blueprint has begun.

The Primary Seven Chakras

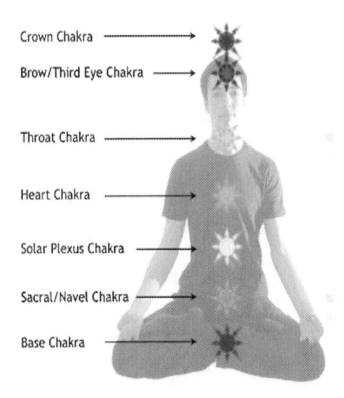

Crown Chakra

Brow/Third Eye Chakra

Throat Chakra

Heart Chakra

Solar Plexus Chakra

Sacral/Navel Chakra

Base Chakra

New Crystal Chakra System

The Supreme Creator

The Christ Consciousness

The Intergalactic Gateway

The Stellar Gateway

The Soul Star

Seven Primary Chakras + Five New Chakras

The Earth Star

The Dolphin Matrix

The Inner Earth Cities

The Whale Matrix

The Heart of Mother Nature

Re-coding

Re-programming

Re-Attuning

Re-Alignment

Re-Adjusting

Integration

Segment VIII
The Light Bodies

The Light Bodies

Why do we have light bodies and what are they purpose?
They are the light filters, which flow in our natural living state
as energy. They are used to clear, cleanse and release all energy
patterns of the emotional body, the mind, the physical body,
the spiritual body and the ethereal body that we no longer
wish to have. They are interconnected and they operate within
the confines of the specific state of being.

<u>Mind/Mental Body:</u> You start with your mind and the ego,
and apply the new thought recoding patterns. You are in the
process of re-aligning your mind. The recoding of light
language begins through the mind. You will have to move
aside as will your ego, as this process will ask you to stay
centered in your heart. As mentioned with the ascension
process you are moving out of the emotional, ego, physical
based parameters. As you re-train your thinking processes, it
will start the alignment process of both hemispheres of your
brain. Your left and right brain hemispheres are going to be
re-organized separately. While going through the ascension
process, it is normal to feel one side out of sync during your
re-organization process as the decoders of light language are
being integrated, as the other hemisphere takes over briefly.

The left side relates to cognitive reasoning, logic, sorting out
and processing ideas and thoughts. It is normal to have short-
term memory while this is going. You are being given the
chance to relax and work with the right spiritual side for a
while. It is normal to feel like you just want to be quiet, still,
mediate, and spend time outdoors with nature.

Patience is asked of ourselves and of our light counsel who are helping us through our changes. While you are integrating the new thought patterns, you can work on releasing and balancing karma through dream states, meditation, and earthly matters. Your mind never stops processing, acknowledging, accepting and releasing the old patterns of thinking.

You will become more increasing aware of your thoughts and thought energy patterns. You will have inner wisdom of your past lives, karma and your awareness of your choices. This awareness will assist with you with your understanding of the integration of light language decoders. It will become clearer and easier to change your direction of your thoughts towards feeling and listening to your true alignment of your heart and divine source.

When you have balanced the left side of your brain, which is your cognitive side, you switch over to the right side and work on your spiritual mind. You begin to feel energized to do earthly duties, work, and be with family and friends and work on your goals.

The right side of the brain maybe cloudy or fuzzy, with a feeling of being in limbo and questioning your belief systems and meditation may be difficult to do. Better to just walk in nature, listen to music, and take care of *you* more. Do not worry if you feel separated form God; you are not, behold your faith and patience. You are simply clearing out old to make way for new.

This is a good time for planting seeds, ideas of growth cleaning, organizing, pampering you and resting.

The re-training and re-aligning of your mind will take its own time cannot rush this one at all no matter what! So enjoy the peace of not engaging in your head for a while.

The Emotional Body: How do we clear lower energies and emotions in the emotional body? Most of us have never been taught to do this at an earlier age. Society does not give much credence to mental health professionals. Consequently, when we do try, we may experience confusion because we are not familiar with the stages of release of painful emotions and experiences on a conscious level and therefore it takes longer to move through our mental and emotional bodies. For many, this leads to feelings of frustration and they just give up.

However, when we give up, we do so at a price. Remember that the third realm is ego, emotions and physical illusions. A spiritual light system was not set up because this was not our original intention of being. Humanity set up the mental and psychological institutions to manage and help individuals who are not able to cope with the over load of these parameters.

When conflicts remain unresolved, their associated emotions remain, creating energetic imbalances in the body on the physical level that lead to illness. On the mental level, they can create bipolar disorders and, in some cases, severe depression.

On the emotional level, they lead us to act out either in destructive ways such as raging, or in covert ways, using passive and or aggressive behaviour. All of these things are destructive to our personal relationship with our inner essence, not to mention our relationships with others and with our God connection.

In undertaking the clearing of the emotional body, we have the tools to identify what the cause or root of the issue is and how we can handle it responsibly as we make choices.

The following are suggested steps to help identify and handle each feeling you have so you can clear emotional toxics from yourself.

Suggested Steps:

1. What are you feeling?
2. How do you react?
3. How can you handle this better?
4. Let out your feelings in healthy ways.
5. Look at where the emotion originated.
6. If it is your emotion, be responsible of it.
7. Love yourself enough to forgive you and let it go.
8. Seek professional help if you or someone you know needs it.

The Physical Body: This is the vessel of mutual relationship to all other light bodies, your chakras, your spiritual blueprint, with Mother Earth, with the Universe and God.
In order to reach your next level in evolution it is important to remember to do periodic house cleaning, clearing and releasing within your emotional body, and physical body.

The physical body you occupy will make you aware of what needs to go, cleared up and released. It is important to understand that you will feel these energies within your physical body because it needs your awareness of things being felt, or experienced which will tell you are on the right track; you are getting through your stuff.

You will know what thinking patterns must go as well as the behaviours patterns associated with these. You will feel them physically. For example, experiencing love and anger and the sensations associated with these, will be felt within your heart center. The physical body reacts to these feelings. They can even be stored within your system as feelings of well being or dis-ease.

The more align to love and complete well being, the better you will feel and adapt to the new changes to come. If you hold lower energy and negativity within your physical being they will create blockages, dis-ease and they will mirror your life experiences. These need to be released because it only delays where you wish to be. What you think and feel creates your life.

The necessary experiences that you create are lessons of teaching and understanding in order to become completely healthy and experience well being. The physical body needs proper care and loving attention, because it works in unison with your emotional, spiritual and ethereal bodies, no separation of these. It is important to know the effects of stress, diet, dis-ease, resting, and doing things in moderation.

Your physical body will let you know what is going on, because it is working along side with your light bodies, chakras, and enabling you to carry out your physical earth duties.

It is important to listen and pay attention to what your physical body is experiencing. The key is to recognize what is being created, what is happening and what you should do to bring harmony and balance within.

The physical body knows how to get rid of emotional toxins and physical toxins to bring balance within the spiritual and ethereal bodies. Throughout your ascension process you will go through an emotional, or physical purging and cleansing process to achieve your true alignment with your heart and with divinity. This process will affect and change the endocrine system, nervous system, pituitary system, cardiovascular system, the circular system, and the energy light system. The purging process is uncomfortable and similar to having flu.

It will run its course to clean, clear and release lower energies out of your body. You may experience this many times throughout your process as a necessary component of releasing stuff that you are having a hard time dealing with either in one or all of your light bodies. Think of it as a flu gift to help you through your stuff. Not pleasant but needed. It does pass when you have cleared your stuff.

The physical body does much of the inner work with these subsystems to keep us healthy so we can carry out our earthly duties. While we work on our light bodies simultaneously, we are working together with our physical body. When you put effort, time and attention to your physical well being, the rewards will be amazing. These results will enhance your spiritual well-being and you will progress in your soul's evolution.

Spiritual endurance and patience brings understanding of how everything connects with each other to bring balance and harmony. We can put everything into perspective and begin working, aligning, and releasing that which no longer serves God and us.

<u>The Spiritual Body:</u> This light body knows when you are doing your house cleaning. It knows you are going through your chosen teaching and learning experiences. It knows you are putting things together and that you are making sense of everything within you. The spiritual body signals the emotional and the physical body to clean up. Before you get to the final RNA and DNA blueprint process, you must have completed and gone through all of the previous preparation of these segments.

Once you have cleared these the new DNA will change your physical body, but not without the spiritual body's permission. Think of it this way, would you mix old and new together. Your new light body will not accept you like this. Only becoming of pure heart and mind will your physical vessel become attune through your original spiritual light body.

You will have gentle reminders of the love that you are and acknowledgements and tests of your true heart intentions. God and your heart know your true purpose and once you are consciously aware of both, will you understand the magnitude of this as it unfolds for you.

The spiritual light body becomes refined clearer light and you come to the point of realizing there is more to life other than the material and physical. You are now allowing yourself to become open to infinite expressions of pure energies that are available to us. We have guides, teachers, and spiritual counsels all helping us to move forward.

It takes patience, love, surrender and trust with your process, as it takes an enormous commitment of change. Your focus and perception will change.

You can ask for assistance to lift things that are not serving you anymore; just be very specific about what. It is important to surrender to what God and you have agreed to fulfill. God knows your spirit, soul, heart and entrusts your commitments to understanding to the past, present and new contracts you chose and choose.

Now is a good time to pause and reflect on what you have done, cleared, processed and understood before heading any further into the next stages. If you are not ready emotionally, mentally, physically, or spiritually it is because you still have to move through understanding, accepting and clearing within you before you can move on. There is no right or wrong; it is all divine timing for you.

I know this is a lot to comprehend and experience as you go through the transitions. I have gone through my own rapid ascension process in the last several years. I have had enormous changes and adjustments in a short span because I chose to do this with my purpose. No matter what experience, hurt, loss, or karma, we are never separate from God's Love. God holds us, with unconditional love for infinity, even when we cannot pray, or want to be comforted, or we feel alone in this midst of our trials and tribulations.

We have many types of learning and becoming better in many ways that are unique to each of us. An important key to remember is that God has greater expectations and dreams for each one of us. The key to realizing this understanding is by tapping into the silence, peace and trust.

Silence

Peace

Trust

Behold

Present

Honest

Segment IX
The Effects of Light Energy Activations

The Effects of Light Energy Activations

Our planet has been going through a transformation shift to a finer lighter frequency since the nineteen eighties. She is a living moving energy system that wants to birth to her full glory. All inhabitants on this planet who reside within her energy fields will also experience this realignment. First, what many are experiencing naturally, as the planet undergoes her transformation, is what is termed the creation of the light planet. Second, since many are enthusiastic and joyous at these changes, I would like to cover practical things that we can consciously do to build and increase the light quotient in our own bodies.

Realigning ourselves to God's light and changing our vibration frequency will activate and accelerate this process. The process of transition to God's light is a gradual one. We are not matter one day and pure light the next. Our energy fields are continuously absorbing pure light and realigning gradually.

Creation of the light body is due to our planet's current transition process and the repositioning of ourselves within the Universe. The light body is gradually changing through the transmutation of our emotional and physical bodies as it absorbs more Universal light. The following information describes the actual physical process and common symptoms as this change occurs.

We are all evolving and absorbing light at our own pace. Some souls are consciously working with these changes and so their transmutation is quicker. Others are unaware of this, but are absorbing this light, and will eventually feel the changes.

There are souls who are aware of this process with our planet and the Universe simultaneously. I will classify this as your creation of density layers within you and the illusionary veils covering you.

I would like to point out that as you drop the density layers you have created over aeons, the veils of illusion and feeling separate fade away as well. With each releasing and dropping of the emotional, physical, karmic and spiritual densities the veils of illusions we created with these will lift. As you become aware of what densities and what veils you have created, each one will drop and lift to continuously reveal your inner light, truth, joy, and understanding while you are on your journey.

I would like to state wherever you are in releasing and finding the truth in god's light, it is perfectly fine to have your state of being and awareness just right for you. You are choosing to be where and exactly how you wish to be.

The Emotional Layers- These are the layers that you have created of how you emotionally perceive yourself, others and situations around you. Your primary focus must be you first in order to understand how you emotionally have carried yourself up until now. What are your perceptions of how you react emotionally to yourself?

As you become aware of these, you change your emotional awareness of you. This then naturally shifts to how you emotionally perceive others and your emotional perceived responses given back to you.

I would suggest writing how you feel about yourself, others and your life situations very carefully now.

If you are keeping a journal, you may have already written parts of this along your progression.

1. How you feel about yourself now?
2. Important relationships for you and why?
3. What you are doing now?
4. What is becoming your focus now?

Once you have been able to clear your emotional self to accepting, loving and being your higher self this will change how you perceive yourself, others. You will find it is easier to be emotionally detached from situations and circumstances that once kept you in full focus. Once you can do this, it will become second nature for you. It is like breathing air. Do you think about doing this?

Your emotions will change first for you, other people and your life choices will change around you. As you do this the emotional densities within you will drop you will feel you can finally release these. You may find that during these emotional detachments it can be painful or immensely joyful. It is happening to clear you emotionally. You will experience your specific emotions to release these and it is important to allow yourself to express them.

The Physical Layers- These are the barriers or blocks placed by you within your physical body. These can be emotional, physical, karmic or spiritual in nature. Your conscious awareness and pin pointing exactly what they are and where is part of this process of releasing and realigning your physical body to carry your true inner light. Your physical body can hold many types of energies, it can store and hide these too. Your job is to become aware of what is what and where everything is in balance and of harmony.

Keeping harmonious energies and releasing that which no longer serves you and God. You will feel lighter and more light will begin to flow through you.

Karmic or Past lives Layers- You will be able to fully understand and see your life times and remember key lessons. This can happen through your dreams and your conscious awareness in meditative thought moments. Your gift of psychic awareness and or intuition given to you will allow you to accomplish this wondrous facet of doing reconnect healing while you are releasing these. You may have people or situations in this lifetime that you will finally know how to apply your learnt wisdom to clear them. Karma is stored within the emotional, physical and ethereal layers you will sense where these are eventually.

You will know if karma is cleared by the choices, situations and people that come into your life as you go through this. You may even start to feel a sense of relief at what you are clearing and accomplishing.

The Veils of Illusion – Your mind and thought processes have created these which have suited you while you have been existing in the emotional and physical realm. As you move beyond these confines of illusion, you will align yourself more to your true higher self. Your purpose is in alignment with God's light. You have the choice to accept what God has for you. Each new change you have, feel, experience you are to trust, behold your faith, be patient and surrender. There will be moments when these veils will lift gently so you can understand more. You will naturally question all of your beliefs and values.

Part of this process is releasing all that you thought you believed in because it is illusion that you have created. Your true inner light will align more with God's light and with universal wisdom. As each veil is lifted, you will drop a layer of density moving more into a higher state of lightness and peace.

Your perceptions of you will change and it will change your environment around. You may feel disconnected from your former self, and your choices will reflect your changed perspective of life. You may feel disconnected from some people while you understand and respect their chosen path. Your life as you have known it will transform as you step into your uniqueness of who you really are.

With each conscious choice you make to honour your inner light, God will give you moments of peace and inner clarity. You will begin to feel your heart's awareness that opens to greater expansion of wisdom with your life and all life.

I cannot say what your ascension process will be for you because that is between you and God. We are all unique and so will your process be. You will feel you have changed and your whole perspective on life will change. You will also be aware now you cannot hold any negativity within you. Just be much aware of your thoughts, awareness and choices you will be asked of now.

You will naturally know how to think and perceive, as it becomes second nature for you. As with all things, we practise until we feel we have achieved our goal. Like a child, they discover their senses and the uniqueness of themselves with experiences and choices.

This is the same with this process, we have the unique experience of re-discovering ourselves. What actually has happened is that much of humanity is still asleep within their hearts.

We are being given opportunities to awaken, experience, remember the inner heart light and gift. Some people are aware of these changes around us and within. What is puzzling to many is how do we remember our true divinity?

It takes a change and commitment to personally and spiritually take responsibility for all that you have been, have done, and what you are willing to let of and change with your heart awareness of pure intention.

It slowly has been happening throughout your past lives and is evident by your present choices. The most important message is, are you aware of your inner heart light? Once the understanding is felt, we know it to be true. You have an inner conscious connection that seeks to know more.

A childlike wonder shows your light and God's grace through you. In retrospective, the same as a parent looks and feels love and hope with their child. It is not unlike that of our heavenly father who shows unconditional love and hope for all his children.

Humanity is gently being asked and reminded to remove the veils of illusion, which have distorted the true nature of perception and life. Where is the heart of humanity as a whole? It is through the realizations of dropping illusions, and densisties, the light is becomes more apparent as veils lift.

Change

Commitment

Consistent

Open

Respectful

Awaken

Segment X
The Re-Connective Process

The Re-Connective Process

We each have twelve matrix strands of DNA; ten of these
strands have been re-coded and re-built. You have been going
through your ascension process of clearing and releasing
emotionally and physically with your light body. Your light
body is connecting to the higher states of consciousness, and
your twin higher self while your heart is re-aligned.

While you have been under going your transformation, you
have attained a new awareness of these connections and are
mastering your progressive learning process with a better
understanding of the magnitude of your inner core light. Your
light body has the ability to support multidimensional
consciousnesses and create light bridges that are making
connections with the levels of consciousness as you become
aware of what is happening to you and why.

Having a multidimensional connection is our natural state of
light; we have forgotten it as we were living within the
confines of the emotions, ego and physical. Your new task is
to use and understand how your light bodies work, so you can
finally release that which no longer serves God and you.

Realigning, reconnecting and activating our ten strands of
DNA re-coding are the processes by which we attain that
state. When we move into a lighter state of being, our psychic
and intuitive abilities are more apparent and we can feel more
of our heart connection. We can hear, see and communicate
through the heart with light. Are you conscious of the changes
and connections within you? Are you becoming more aware
of your changing dream states?

We have the wisdom of how to remember how to use our consciousness to connect with heart and God. We all have this ability, God gave us many gifts he wants us to hear his light within us and to share his love.

At this level, your ten new matrix strands of DNA along with your two connected matrix strands are re-aligned above your crown. Because the new DNA is transparent, it can be simultaneously realigned, reconnected and activated. This means that your ten DNA strands are simultaneously realigned at the top of your crown: reconnected into your crown chakra and reactivated so that life force energy flows through them again. Once all your ten DNA strands are rewoven to your crown, your team of Light Engineers work is nearly complete.

The final two matrixes, which are the divine and twin higher self, will be connected at the final stages of ascension. Your light counsel will continue to watch over you and monitor your twelve-strand reconnection until you reach the frequency needed to activate the reconnection.

The activation of each matrix strand happens in three stages:

1. The Activation of the Crown; you will feel this as a tingling sensation at the Crown.

2. The Activation of the Pineal Glands and the Hypothalamus; this is the Universal translator and translates all messages into your chosen language. Messages are received as frequency thought forms. Many are complete with feelings, pictures and light language. Some have only one or two of these. The hypothalamus provides you with the identity of the sender.

3. The Activation of the Light Body; the light body receives Universal Light Language as coded messages. You will learn to identify the senders after receiving for a while.

Once the hypothalamus is activated the recoding process of your DNA and your new chart is also completed. Validation of this is seeing matter change around and with you.

You will be able to see light patterns, hear light frequencies and tones, you will be able to see the light fields around and in people's energy fields. You will be much aware that you cannot hold any lower energies, lower frequencies within you or around you. You will feel the essence of your heart light much more and be able to see it flow from you. You will be able to daily receive and send light messages from your heart.

As you go through this try and remember to be aware of how you are feeling mentally, emotionally, physically now? Are you seeing, feeling and aware of your changes? It is important to acknowledge everything you are going through systematically.

You will feel again each reminder of your present state and you will progress daily into your mastering of your new light bodies.

There still will be moments that you will feel the need to silence out that whish is distortion for you. Each step is required as you are stepping into your essence of shared divinity light through the awareness of simply being through your heart.

Every step you take will bring you into that which God has for you, all that is asked, is to trust you are being guided.

There will be experiences that will offer you choices and you will be tested of your wisdom repeatedly.

A great deal of this ascension process is of heart choices and realizing the awareness of your choices that bring you closer and into your divine purpose. Each soul is sacred and is part of the divine plan. There is no right or wrong, just what is right for you. I believe God shows us unconditionally what we choose by our awareness of where we are and what we have learnt thus far.

Honour thy self-true and accept others in the same way as the Universal way of life. We will know this through this re-connective process of source and ourselves.

An undeniable truth will surface into your conscious state and it will begin to flow through your heart center as you understand more of what we are, what we are part of, and respecting each light soul as part of a the divine design.

This process of reconnection to your new awareness will touch each new chakra that has been integrated into you. You will feel it become apart of you and closer to understanding how life is created, and what effects change and beginning.

You will feel the lesser denser effects of others and their choices more intensely and personally. This depends where they are, you may feel the need to disconnect the energies of learnt experiences and feelings of those around you.

You will feel the light, love and understanding that come with this in time. You will respect and understand each has a path uniquely chosen just for them.

Within

Without

Experiencing

Discovering

Discernment

Astuteness

Segment XI
Light and Frequency Re-Activations

Light and Frequency Re-Activations

Your new inner core will be connected to your heart light center. Your heart will become aware of this new activation that has happened within you. You will not feel like the same person you once were. You may hear the changes of light within you and around you, and you may see these as well.

Your ten matrix strains are established and reconnected to your crown at a comfortable pace, which will allow you to make the necessary emotional and physical adjustments. Your light bodies will require periodic cleaning and checkups. You will naturally feel light energy moving through you. You will be very much aware of everything inside of you and will know all your connections as they are gently done.

As you are making your connections it is normal to feel heat inside, you may even feel liquid fluid moving through out your body. You may feel your body vibrating inside as the light energies are new. Now is the time to allow your physical body the time it needs to adjust to your new changes.

There will times where you are full of energy and at other times feel the need to be quiet, rest and just be. It is important to listen to how you feel now, because your heart and body will tell you; be gentle with yourself now. As you make the connections, every part of you will realign and interweave in divine pure light. As you, become now more aware of how your light bodies are working, you will know how to clear them and maintain balance. You have achieved the awareness of being able to maintain your light bodies of all lower emotional and physical detachments, which in the past concealed your inner heart light.

You may periodically have to under go a purging process as to maintain your inner balance and harmony. You are to be responsible and be an active willing participant in maintaining your new light system, your light heart center.

You will find throughout your ascension process that your values, beliefs, attitudes and outlook on life is new, fresh, lighter, and peaceful; you will feel very content and happy with the new you ! Trust yourself and the process you are going through and remain open to all possibilities, choices and perceptions that will unfold for you.

As long as we all live by the honour of our true light, we create more peace and more light and it naturally flows to all creation. Life is to create light and evolution of wisdom is a natural progressive process.

Once you have this knowing you are connected. A strong intuitive sense of trust and leap of faith will be asked of you as you live from your heart. You will make your life changes in accordance to begin your new contract of service. You will feel softer, lighter, and clearer and love yourself more than you ever could imagine. You will understand, feel and appreciate everything within you and around you. You will be given your time and space to enjoy your new awareness of yourself before you choose to progress ahead through grace.

You will feel free to be the new you as you live from your full heart of love and service to others. The gift of your change will allow you to feel unconditional love more with your heart, God and all life, in a way that is incredible.

Milieu

Wisdom

Resilience

Focus

Aware

Surrender

Segment XII
The Twelve Matrixes

The Twelve Matrixes

The process of ascension involves many areas and levels that we are simultaneously processing through with the gift of conscious connection of our unique process. Our inner twelve matrixes have been re-built and re-coded. They are re-connected and by our light team. This is based on what we have chosen with pure intent through the heart and for our soul's evolution.

Throughout the passages of key increments of knowledge and re-connective healing, you have learnt that the light bodies filter all that which we release emotionally, physically and of the mind. The twelve segments of this book are your twelve matrixes or levels that you are changing about you. I have mentioned the matrixes several times throughout these passages and I hope you now understand the scope and magnitude of what the ascension process is.

Ten of your matrix strands have under gone the transformation process. The two remaining matrixes that are of the divine connection and your twin higher self will merge through your light system into your heart center at the appropriate time of your ascension. Once your ascension process happens, you will be given time to adjust and begin to understand the magnitude of your commitment as light.

The twelve matrixes of this process of ascension are all about you mastering your light with wisdom. The twelve matrixes are of your re-defined focused light intention purified. This only will unfold with your awareness of God's light while applying the wisdom of the universal fundamentals. Only through the passage of your heart will you master light and wisdom through God's grace.

There is no specific frame of time reference for your ascension. It is all divine light and your choices given and made towards God's light.

The Harmonic Convergence gateway started in the late nineties where the energy has been available for the shift into a fifth dimensional consciousness while in a physical body. There are souls who have already been through their process. For each soul, ascension will continue until you are ready, to move more towards light.

The beginning of the ascension is when a person is consciously aware of how to live each moment through their creative continuous masterpiece of love balance with all and for all. I would like to say that those who are within groups with individuals who are aware of the light and the changes we are going through, one or more might go through the ascension process. It is actually beneficial to all in the group to witness this, as it will help others understand what has taken place.

This ascension process for our planet started in the late eighties, we are now realizing that as mother nature has consciously connected to specific souls for the need of her change to begin. This is when she began to shed and cleanse layers of impurities while simultaneously accepting the new light infusion. This explains the weather, natural elements of air, fire, earth and water creating the conditions of her release and cleansing process. Planetary shifts have been ushered in by a series of light infusion processes.

Gateways are energetic conduits of frequencies opened from higher dimensions. These conduits bring through the energies necessary to pattern mass consciousness, change planetary vibrations, and to change dimensional frequencies.

A gateway requires the assistance of the many beings on higher dimensional frequencies to create it and to refine the energies for the specified purpose. The purpose of a gateway and the frequencies is the domain of the Light Hierarchy Counsels. There are souls on this planet who aware of these gateways, those who are the gatekeepers and those who are the wisdom keepers.

The Harmonic Convergence gateway allowed the beginnings of becoming aware of non-linear time as we are moving into the moment of Now. The veils of separation and duality are thinning. The Universal aspect of life is moving closer for all life.

As you are coming to terms with yourself, as you process and transform your karma, your conscious states are aligning to match the new you. You are clearing and realigning your light bodies the emotional, physical and spiritual.

You will learn to understand how these work in unison with each other, as you are changing through light and form to merge into your light body.

The "Now of Ascension", is when you begin to experience a new spiritual blueprint of your light, and you understand and feel a unique connection foe you, each other, the Universe and God.

I hope you will to begin to comprehend the understanding of the Unification Laws and the principles that are available to us now. They are the fundamentals of understanding the light and unconditional love. God knows your heart, your spirit, your choices, your thoughts and your direction towards the light.

You will be introduced into your new life changes that will surface within your being. You are to take the time and patience to feel and perceive through your heart's awareness. Your light counsel will then allow you to feel the connections made through your crown and then integrate them into whole state of light awareness by activating those through your heart.

This part of your ascension is unique and special for you. You will experience more with time the understanding of what will unfold for you and why. I cannot describe this any further as it is totally experienced uniquely in the way you have chosen it to unfold. You will experience a profound sense of gratitude and wisdom of awareness and purity connected with God.

You may have experienced changes with your guides, and your light counsel, your dream states, and your focus. Your perceptions are changing through learnt wisdom of all that you have been through thus far. Your goals have changed and you are now learning how to become your focus of intention with light and wisdom.

Mastering your light with all the responsibilities of totally honouring who you are will become your focus. Wisdom has taught you valuable lessons of self and others. We are asked to respect the light, honour thy true light and allow God to handle the rest. What remains is gratitude with grace.

Oneness

Silent

Lightness

Vigour

Valiant

Honour

Parting Thoughts

Parting Thoughts

This book is an invitation, a choice, and a gift, a personal and spiritual process to journey through and toward God's light. What ever you have been seeking to understand about you, the essence of life, the light of spirit, you will witness this by God's grace onto you by your awareness through choice, change and wisdom.

There is much talk and speculation about what is "ascension"? It is a spiritual process of seeking your true light and the journey with our soul to God's light. We are simply choosing where we wish to be by our conscious awareness of our spiritual growth and the choices within that awareness. It will happen naturally as trees bud their seeds.

Throughout time, and non-linear time the conscious awareness to move forward to God's light is available to all souls and every choice is honoured. These segments of knowledge are to enlightenment your heart into a wondrous conscious state of simply honouring your intention of your light on your soul's journey. There is no right or wrong only light and unconditional love for all.

"Those that wish to stay where they are will."
"Those that wish to change will."
"Those that wonder, joy in the discoveries."
"Those seek understanding, it shall unfold within."
"Your choices reflect you, the wisdom of your light."

Be still to hear, feel, seek, discover and understand your light within. May you find that what you seek and share through your heart with Joy, Peace, Love, Wisdom and Gratitude!

Gratitude With Grace

No sunrise…no sunset…there is light…
The stillness of my heart is the wisdom of the universe…
A twinkle of remembrance…
The serene of reflective glistening sparks…
Reciprocate unconditional love…
The mantra of vibrational tones…
The light and precision of grace and wisdom…
A moment of understanding and choice…
Teachings of the heart and lessons learnt…
A shared hug and tears wiped…
The gentle light of innocence…
The fruits of your endeavours…
The radiance of your spirit…
The Universal Sonata…
God's endowment of tomorrow to come…
I am illuminated…
"Glory to God"